The Student Teacher Quotes

By: Simene' Walden

The Student Teacher Quotes by Simene' Walden

Published by The Student Teacher

P.O. Box 813

SAVAGE, MD 20763

© 2017 by Simené Walden

All rights reserved. Copyright under Berne Copyright Convention, Universal Copyright Convention, and Pan-American Copyright Convention. No part of this book may be reproduced, stored in a retrieval system, or transmitted in any form, or by any means, electronic, mechanical, photocopying, recording or otherwise, without prior permission of the author.

For permission contact: thestudentteacher17@gmail.com

Editor: The Student Teacher

Front Cover Photograph: Bella Dawn Photography

Graphic Design: Ghanipixels

First Printing, November 8, 2017

Printed in the United States of America

ISBN: 978-0-9997987-0-6

If you are interested in special quantity discounts for bulk purchases please contact the author directly via email.

Table of Contents

Preamble 1

About the Author 3

Testimonials from "Standing On His Words: Prayers and Devotionals Every Educator Can Pray" 5

Standing On His Words Courses and Seminars 7

Testimonials from "Spiritual Combat" 11

Spiritual Combat Workshop 13

Speaker Topics 15

The Student Teacher Quotes 17

Words of Gratitude 114

Preamble

A quote can be defined as a phrase or saying that someone uses often. I do not and have not used these quotes often but I use them when necessary. I hope you will find some of them, if not all, fitting, helpful, encouraging, and uplifting. Feel free to use them and them share them with others. Don't forget to tag me in any of your pose on social media.

About the Author

A native of North Carolina, Simene' (Sim ma nae) Walden grew up in Northampton County, North Carolina where she attended Northampton County Public Schools. During the initial five years after graduating high school, she pursued her education at three different colleges only to find herself back where she started: Fayetteville State University. In 2004, Simené graduated with a Bachelor of Arts degree in English & Literature from Fayetteville State University. Ten years later, she obtained her Masters of Arts degree in Christian Studies with an emphasis on Youth Ministry from Grand Canyon University.

Simené also known as "The Student Teacher", was given that name by the Holy Ghost on June 7, 2016. She is a teacher by vocation but is always in a place of learning something new that will catapult her to the next level in her destiny. Simene' is a teacher, accountability coach, writer, speaker, and an Amazon Best Selling Author. She believes in being teachable and remains in a posture of learning even from those one may not think has anything to offer. Simene' believes that everyone has something to offer. Simené's primary objective is to empower, educate, and equip others as she teaches them everything she has learned.

She actively serves in various ministries in her local church. God's servant openly shares her love for God on her social media sites as well as in the marketplace. Her ministry started on the streets of Washington, DC. She is the Chief Operating Officer of *The Student Teacher,* where she is flooding the Educational System with God's Words of prayer. Simene' is also the author of Standing On His Words: Prayers and Devotions Every Educator Can Pray, Standing On His Words Workbook: Prayers and Devotions Every Educator Can Pray, Spiritual Combat, and My Heart Under A Microscope. Her sixth book Youth In Crisis will be released in January.

Contact the author:

www.simenewalden.com

thestudentteacher17@gmail.com

https://www.facebook.com/thestudenteacher

https://www.twitter.com/@simenewalden

https://www.periscope.tv/@simenewalden

https://instagram.com/simenewalden

Mailing Address: P.O. Box 813 Savage, MD 20763

Testimonials from

"Standing On His Words: Prayers and Devotionals Every Educator Can Pray"

Recently, I purchased, Standing on His Words, by Simene' Walden because I was interested in learning about how I could spiritually address many of the challenges within the educational system. From the first prayer, Empowering Educators Through Prayer, I was captivated by the power and passion that was outlined as she exposes the devil in schools across the world! Each prayer addresses the reasons why prayer is important for all of us regardless of whether we are educators, administrators, or parents. As an administrator, there is a prayer that directly speaks to preparing my heart to address the needs of my schools in a professional Christ-like way as opposed to the way of the world. My favorite is chapter called, Prayers for Intercessors Praying for the Educational System. This chapter is call to action for all people to confront the specific challenges close to their hearts and intercede through prayer. As a mother, I have prayed several devotions from this book over my child daily, and I am looking forward to using it in conjunction with my Bible as there is specific scripture that that accompanies each devotion. I cannot wait to see the manifestation of God's power through these prayers! Thank you, Simene' for writing this book to encourage us as adults to pray for our children and ourselves to be better stewards over the God's Kingdom. I stand with you in the movement of #praying4schools through #StandingonHisWords.

(Alma, Amazon Review)

Both as an advocate for Moms in Prayer, an Educator and a mom myself, I find this resource to be invaluable! The power of prayer is monumental and we need it now more than ever! Excellent guide!

(Anita, Amazon Review)

As an educator, I recommend this book to my fellow educator as a reminder of why we do what we do. Get your copy today!

(Aikyna, Amazon Review)

This book is one to not only Read BUT keep out ON your desk!! Soooo many great insights and prayers for sooo many at different stages AND struggles as well!! GREAT reference!!! A Definite book to get for all!!!!!

(Kelly, Amazon Review)

It is good you are sharing your gift with the world, and educators in particular. I haven't read a book on this topic yet. Thanks again.

(Deborah, Colleague)

Standing On His Words Courses and Seminars

Young Adults (17-24)

The Struggle Is Real: Parents Just Don't Understand

Do you often bump heads with your teenager and/or young adult? Do they feel like they are always being corrected for doing something wrong that they actually believe is right? Do they seem lost and frustrated because they want to create the life God has for them, but they have no idea what that is and what that looks like?

If you answered yes to either of these questions, this seminar is for your child!

This seminar will give your child real-solutions to very real problems in a very real and aggressive world. Within this workshop, teenagers and young adults will learn how to perfect the areas of concern in their lives from biblical truths and practical teaching.

The four modules will include the following:

1. How to create a blueprint for your life?
2. How to take the opinions of others and learn from them?
3. How to talk to God and get real-time answers?
4. How to focus on yourself and become the Best YOU?

Adults (25-40)

The Struggle Is Real: People Just Don't Understand

Do you often bump heads with people? Are you criticized about the way you see things and how you live your life? Do you often feel like the people around you do not relate to you and don't understand your viewpoint on many things?

This seminar will give you real-solutions to your very real problems in a very real and aggressive world. In this class, you will learn how to perfect the areas of concern in your life from biblical truths and practical teaching.

The four modules will include the following:

1. How to create a blueprint for your life?
2. How to take the opinions of others and learn from them?
3. How to talk to God and get real-time answers?
4. How to focus on yourself and become the Best YOU?

(Educators, Leaders, Administrators)

Creating a Culture of Collaboration and Respect

As the demands of excellence, production, and results are eminent, do you desire to respect all children regardless of their behaviors and interactions with you? Do you wish to respect and gain respect from fellow colleagues? Do you work in an atmosphere that could use some positive TLC?

In this class, you will learn how to create a place of peace in the environments that seem to be dominated by drama, negativity, and hostility.

The six modules will include the following:

1. How to create a culturally sensitive and affirmative environment?
2. How to create an Educational Environment not mirrored by the image of the Penal System?
3. How to protect yourself from being influenced by the accusations of others?
4. How to minimize distractions in the workforce?
5. How to honestly communicate with others even when angry?

Additional Seminars and Courses Include:

How to avoid "burn out"?

How to have the heart of a teacher and not just the knowledge of one?

Each seminar and course is a 4-hour session that includes the book and all other materials.

For booking inquiries and speaking engagements, please contact the author directly via email @thestudentteacher17@gmail.com.

Additional Books By The Author

Standing On His Words Ebook Available @ **bit.ly/2Stand**

Standing On His Works Print Book Available **@bit.ly/2StandBook**

Standing On His Words Workbook Available **@bit.ly/StandingWB**

Spiritual Combat Print Book Available **@bit.ly/combatprayerbook**

Spiritual Combat EBook Available @ **bit.ly/combatprayer**

My Heart Under A Microscope Available **@bit.ly/heartunderscope**

Testimonials from

"Spiritual Combat"

This book gave me more scriptures to read for my healing and how to fight my enemies. This is a very good read.

(Victoria, Amazon Review)

This is a phenomenal read that will equip you for battle in the spirit realm. This book should be in every Christian soldier's arsenal!

(Brent & Angel Rhodes - Marriage of God, Amazon Review)

Spiritual Combat Workshop

Prayer Board

Does your life look like you envisioned it? Is your life aligning with what a parent, pastor, or prophet has told you? Has the Word failed you or have you failed the Word? Do you even know what the Word says about your situation and your life?

In this class, you will learn how to create the life you want by designing a visual prayer board of your necessities, needs, and desires from God. In this course, you will learn how to apply God's Words to your prayer request to obtain God driven and God given results.

The six modules will include the following:

1. Identifying your necessities, needs, and desires.
2. Finding scripture that answers your prayer request.
3. Gathering pictures that align with your prayer request.
4. Designing your prayer board.
5. How to incorporate the prayer board into your daily life?
6. What do I do once the prayer is answered?

Speaker Topics

- How to have the heart of a teacher?
- The Process Through Perversion
- Help! My Heart Needs Deliverance!
- Are We Free In Secret?
- Learning How To Prioritize
- Words Matter: Speak Life
- Dysfunction Between Mothers and Daughters (How to detect it and overcome it?)
- Do Not Be Ensnared By A Title (How to be free with titles?)
- Fruit Flies: What Happens When You Don't Use Your Gifts?
- From Frustration to Forgiveness
- How The Educational System Reflects The Penal System?
- Extreme Rejection for Divine Acceptance
- The Perfect Sin
- Religion and Relationships
- Same Issues Different Interest
- The Cost of The Anointing
- How Sick Are You? Some are physically sick while others are both physically and spiritually sick.

Simene' Walden's Signature Message

Don't Lose ME

(Do Not Lose Your Morals and Ethics In The Marketplace)

The Speech That Quotes

The Student Teacher Quotes

Don't ask for more if you can not handle what I have already given you. That includes more of my time, my love, my compassion, and my heart. (from God)

_____
_____
_____
_____

Stop trying to prove to people you matter. You do. You absolutely DO MATTER!

_____
_____
_____
_____

Those who have nothing going on will never celebrate someone who does.

_____
_____
_____
_____

If all we read is the world's news, all we will have is a world's view.

_____
_____
_____
_____

Stop telling people all about your success. Some people really are not happy about you nor your success.

_____
_____
_____
_____

Secret envy and secret jealousy makes people hate you and everything you stand for. Their bones are decaying daily because of it.

_____
_____
_____
_____

The Student Teacher Quotes

Everyone has problems. People just may not tell you or post it to a media site. Privacy is a commodity today.

Don't use the Bible to justify sin. Don't use the bible to punish someone else. Use the Bible as a mirror for your own life.

Support and dictatorship are two different things. If you can't support without wanting to take over, take off.

People respond based on what they know. Don't question their response, question what they know.

_____
_____
_____
_____

The type of follower you are will follow you right into the leadership position you have; if you make it that far. Be kind. Be consistent. Be teachable. Be humble and respect those in authority over you. Reciprocity is coming your way. Are you willing to accept what is going to be exchanged?

_____
_____
_____
_____

Limit success talk with unsuccessful people. They will soon call your acknowledgement of hard work bragging.

_____
_____
_____
_____

The Student Teacher Quotes

Being helpful sometimes is a crutch for others.

_____
_____
_____
_____

What one may think is helpful can very well be detrimental to another person.

_____
_____
_____
_____

Some people don't mind you growing, as long as you don't out grow them.

_____
_____
_____
_____

Simene' Walden

Don't allow someone else to make you think your success is boring or minute. Your success is your success. Their inability to see it is their own blindness. Allow them to stay in the dark until they can handle the light shining through you.

_____

_____

_____

_____

Stand your ground. Believe what you believe and don't back down because a majority may disagree.

_____

_____

_____

_____

Study and implement what works for you and your relationship. Then be satisfied and secure knowing that it works for you and not anyone else's. After you study it, implement, and become secure in your own relationship. Watch it grow into something beautiful.

_____

_____

_____

_____

The Student Teacher Quotes

When you get pride and ego out of the way, doors can open with opportunities of greatness and success.

_____

_____

_____

_____

Don't reassign the assignment God has given you because of your own insecurities. -Kimberly Byrd

_____

_____

_____

_____

Your love does not make it right. God's love does.

_____

_____

_____

_____

People don't mind you walking in their shadows. They mind when you become a spotlight.

Don't wait to go up to humble yourself. You may never make it.

The same way you have been called up, you can very well be called down. - Nathan Simmons

The Student Teacher Quotes

Don't respond publicly to what someone replied to you privately.

Deal with it all; or none at all.

Ministry should not cost you your marriage.

Don't allow the rejection of other people, constructs, organizations, or systems to make you reject yourself.

___

All support is not godly support but if you never support, please shut up.

___

Let your praise be as loud as your critique.

___

The Student Teacher Quotes

You can't help those who shut you out.

Your situation doesn't change your identification.

Don't allow people to make you feel bad for taking care of you.

May your aggravation move you into action.

Simene' Walden

What are you doing with the dash that will go in the middle of your birth and death date?

_____

_____

_____

_____

May the dash on your tombstone hold more weight than how you left this earth.

_____

_____

_____

_____

People will hate you for being something they are not.

_____

_____

_____

_____

The Student Teacher Quotes

Do not allow the deception of unity to wreck havoc in your own relationships.

Many people stay stuck in their past because it's easy and familiar. They know what to expect in their past. Fear grips the heart of many who are have no idea what to expect in their future, so they refuse to go. Take a chance on success. After all, you've tried failure too many times.

Some people want you to change your business to suit them. May your business change the way they want to be suited.

People will convince you to overlook the sins of others because they want you to overlook them either before they do it or reveal to you that they already have.

___

You can edit a picture but you can't edit your past.

___

Don't allow the fear of responsibility to keep you from buying a home.

The Student Teacher Quotes

Friends stand with you when everyone else is stoning you. Friends stand with you when everyone else sits on you.

_____

_____

_____

_____

If people are inconsistent in their own lives, don't expect them to be consistent in yours.

_____

_____

_____

_____

Expose your failures to yourself so you can stop failing.

_____

_____

_____

_____

Simene' Walden

May God turn your wilderness into a paradise.

You will not be the right fit in every place, but you will be the perfect fit in the right place.

Don't allow politics to determine your faith. Don't allow politics to dictate how much you believe or do not believe in God.

The Student Teacher Quotes

Don't be too quick to run to those who are running from others.

Motivational speaking in the pulpit is demonic activity.

Don't allow the order of your services to be so structured that you order God right out of them.

Women in ministry get hurt the most. Women stop uniting in dress and forsaking to unite in the spirit.

May your gifts and talents not bring you before men and be rejected by God.

Be free from the burdens you carry.

The Student Teacher Quotes

Prayers are like shotguns. The more you fire them off, the more it kills the enemy and takes him down.

_____
_____
_____
_____

May you be a generational curse breaker, legacy maker, and wealth creator.

_____
_____
_____
_____

The quality of love you have will depend on the amount of God's love that's in it.

_____
_____
_____
_____

Simene' Walden

The youth are in a crisis. If you take Christ to the youth, their crisis will bow to Him.

_____
_____
_____
_____

May my failures keep you from falling.

_____
_____
_____
_____

If your sins come in cycles, break the cycle and create a new one.

_____
_____
_____
_____

The Student Teacher Quotes

Don't lie on people and then run.

Don't be hoodwinked by all the "conscious" talk. If you're not hooked to a ventilator, you are conscious. The talk should be around the awareness of your consciousness in which you talk.

The Lord will turn up the heat and even change the thermostat until he gets the room (your spirit) right for his desired temperature.

Sing to God. Stop singing about God.

___

Find a clean vessel who can cover you until you come out.

___

When people switch up on you, sometimes it's not about you. They are deciding who they will be for that day, or who they need to be in order to deal with who showed up in front of them.

The Student Teacher Quotes

Spiritual wisdom is the birth canal for maturity.
Kimberly Byrd

_____

_____

_____

_____

The Word you live by is the Word that will not die.

_____

_____

_____

_____

Politics do not determine your faith.

_____

_____

_____

_____

Wake your satanic self up!!!

___

While you are being awaken, spiritually detox.

___

Do not repeat the wrongs of others.

___

The sword you carry will keep certain people away, while it will attract others. Who are you attracting?

___

The Student Teacher Quotes

Sabotage is not doing someone a favor.

_____
_____
_____
_____

It is easy to forget your God when he dies. Thank God that Jesus still lives.

_____
_____
_____
_____

When someone tells you not to tell anyone, does that mean not to tell someone they know?

_____
_____
_____
_____

Just because someone doesn't know another person, does not make it right to tell them their business.

Leaders pay a hefty price. Think about the titles you are aspiring to accumulate. Work in the role before ever having the title because if you need one to do the work, you do not need that title. Leaders pay a hefty price for that which you desire.

Be careful of those who befriend you just to keep track of what others are saying about them.

The opposite of low self-esteem is pride. Those who operate in one is usually battling the other.

There will always be one from your generation or time who is the forerunner. They speak for you because you may be too shy, too intimidated, or too ashamed to speak for yourself. Many people are still bound because they will not tell their testimony. You are not an overcomer; you are undercover.

Relationships end because of two spirits; Jesus or satan. Jesus may use satan to end it, but many times after satan has ended it, we cry out to Jesus.

Don't allow your family to act like they have the inside scoop on you from your social media post. Remind them that they just found out like everyone else.

___

Your honesty and transparency scares and threatens those who have so many secrets and skeletons.

___

The devil should have to kidnap you and take you to hell because of your unwillingness to voluntarily go.

___

The Student Teacher Quotes

You can hire an attorney to cover up what you have done, but nothing is hidden from God.

___

The best way to counterattack sin is to live a righteous life. Easy right. Try living it.

___

If you get upset with someone over one disagreement, you did not get upset with them over that one disagreement.

You can never be humble before God and never broken.

Be more concerned about losing your place in God than man.

Stop looking for acceptance from satan.

Don't rush the process; study it. After you study it, execute it in your own life.

___

When people change, study and watch the change.

___

Don't allow another person's past to dictate your future.

___

You can hide from people; you just can't hide from God.

When God gives you an assignment, if you refuse to do it, he will relieve you from it.

___

Stop running to the church as a safe haven and run into the shelter of the Most High King.

___

Cut off all demonic attractions.

The Student Teacher Quotes

You can master how to "go live" on social media, but first learn how to "be alive" in your own life.

God ordained appointments aren't always celebrated by man. Mankind's created and chosen appointments, acknowledgements, assignments, or accolades are not necessarily celebrated by God.

The level of sin you compromise determines the level of sin you minimize.

Don't look up in envy; go down in prayer, and then watch God raise you up.

_____
_____
_____
_____

Stop wanting to run into your ex if they are not heading in the same direction as you.

_____
_____
_____
_____

Rightly divide the truth you will live by.

_____
_____
_____
_____

The Student Teacher Quotes

Spiritual viruses spread on contact. If infected, wash thoroughly with the Word of God.

Normal is relative; just be you.

Do you know how many people are bound right now because people look past their sins to gaze at their flesh?

Ministry is the most dangerous job you will ever have. It is the most intense, most concentrated, yet most rewarded career ever. Ministry should be your first job.

_____
_____
_____
_____

Do not focus on the affirmations and need of others that we neglect the affirmations and need from God.

_____
_____
_____
_____

Don't just sing it; live it.

_____
_____
_____
_____

The Student Teacher Quotes

If your word carries no weight in the spirit, my mind carries no worry about it in the natural.

Rain, sleet, hail; Jesus Never Fails!

Your purpose is not found in a job or career; it is found in the kingdom. The kingdom will birth your career.

Instead of being a spiritual slut, be a saint. Instead of spiritually fornicating, forgive. Instead of promoting spiritual prostitution, promote God.

Those who seem the strongest are sometimes the most broken.

Be sure God has called you and told you to do something because when the heat intensifies, you will have to make sure you can stand.

The Student Teacher Quotes

Some people only like fragmented Christians because it makes them seem whole.

Women who are desperate, lose their husbands by encouraging them to do the things that further their insecurities.

Torment torment, reject rejection, and abandon abandonment.

You can not make up for lost time. In fact, there is no such thing as lost time. Time knew where it was going; people just didn't.

Consistency in God will keep the enemy inconsistent in your life.

Receive strategy not just from man but from God.

The Student Teacher Quotes

The world wants a pretty face with no word, while the kingdom seeks the pretty hearts full of substance and meat.

_____
_____
_____
_____

Fear of losing your voice in the world is nothing comparable to losing your voice with God.

_____
_____
_____
_____

You can have a person's job, but you can not have their calling.

_____
_____
_____
_____

Do not keep telling a sinner their lifestyle is pleasing to God. You too can end up in hell for making someone else fall.

Examine those who you think are building blocks. They may just be roadblocks that stand at the entrance of your future.

You do not want a clean body and a dirty spirit. Get that Word and start washing.

The Student Teacher Quotes

Many people struggle with emotional needs that turn into sexual sins.

_____
_____
_____
_____

As the world is turning, keep turning the pages in the bible. #propheciesbeingfulfilled

_____
_____
_____
_____

The method in which you get God to move is through prayer.

_____
_____
_____
_____

When someone is rude and wrong, just laugh at them. God does and then sends them into derision.

Your last sin can very well catch up with you in your present future.

By all means take care of you and take care of you without the expense of mishandling someone else.

The Student Teacher Quotes

Past sins can affect your future promises.

___

Allow people to digest who you are becoming piece by piece.

___

Don't take advice from anyone who only has ideas and critique. Advise them to talk to you when they can produce results starting with themselves.

Simene' Walden

You don't need many; you just need unity.

Watch out for those who name drop "family" when they need you, but disown you with distance when they don't.

Don't take your secrets to the grave. Expose them and set yourself free.

The Student Teacher Quotes

Stop looking for a Word for someone else. Start looking for a Word for yourself.

Just because someone tells you that another person is not right for you, does not mean they are saying the person is bad. They may be saying the person is bad for you and possibly good for someone else.

Tell it all or don't tell it at all.

If your success burns the ears of those that you are telling, change the ear of the one whom you are sharing.

_____

_____

_____

_____

Don't allow people to throw you in the midst of their troubles.

_____

_____

_____

_____

Take advice only from those who have evidence that what they are saying has worked for them.

_____

_____

_____

_____

The Student Teacher Quotes

It's better to ask than to assume.

___

Don't let someone's evil be spoken good of.

___

Fire will get you moving.

___

Either take your testimony to heaven or you will take your test to hell.

Simene' Walden

Stop giving your tale away. Start giving your heart away because the moment you do, your tale will not be so easily accessible.

_____

_____

_____

_____

There is power in the follow up.

_____

_____

_____

_____

Don't change your message because some people leave. Keep your message so the ones that need it will come.

_____

_____

_____

_____

The Student Teacher Quotes

Don't wake up to read the world's news. Wake up and read God's news. Then apply God's news to the world's news. The lesser has to bow to the greater.

___

Don't allow people to try and make you love or live their life. Just live your own.

___

Make your life as integral and authentic as possible.

Don't walk around with your hidden depression exposed.

Don't chase power; chase influence. Influence will make you powerful.

It's ok to confront the errors you see in your friends. If they are your friends, they may not want it, but they will appreciate you.

The Student Teacher Quotes

Ungodly loyalty is still sin. How can you be loyal to what God has instructed you to cut off?

___

You can still be friends with your friends ex if they haven't done anything to you.

___

Lying to win an argument is not only immature and stupid but it's also sin.

Being strong and controlling are not the same. Most people try to control others because they aren't strong.

Make your pain pay you. Say "Pain Pay Me"!!

People address you by the way they see you. Perception becomes your name. If you don't like what they see, change their perception by the way you live and look.

The Student Teacher Quotes

Unchecked negativity makes a person nasty.

_____

_____

_____

_____

A negative and nasty attitude is the formula and recipe for an emotional nightmare.

_____

_____

_____

_____

Plug into the power source before you die.

_____

_____

_____

_____

Parents will spend their last on their child. Investing in yourself makes you much more valuable to your child. Investing in you will be the biggest payment and gift you can ever give your child.

#notonmaterialthings

#emotionalhealth

#spiritualhealth

#physicalhealth

#mentalhealth

_____
_____
_____
_____

That which you say about others may just be your portion.

_____
_____
_____
_____

The Student Teacher Quotes

Sometimes we don't realize how broken we are until God starts to put us back together.

_____

_____

_____

_____

If you think the nastiness of people starts or stops at work, you're wrong. Check their personal life.

_____

_____

_____

_____

Relationships do not change truth, but truth can change relationships.

_____

_____

_____

_____

Don't give people your time who do not value it.

_____
_____
_____
_____

Stop expecting everyone who knows you to support you.

_____
_____
_____
_____

Running a business is not free. If you want anything free, you might want to do it yourself. Even with you doing it, it will cost you something.

_____
_____
_____
_____

The Student Teacher Quotes

Write the book that you want to read and purchases for free.

_____

_____

_____

_____

Celebrating yourself and bragging is two different things. Acknowledge your hard work and celebrate the success the Lord has graced you to accomplish.

_____

_____

_____

_____

Some people want your "did it for a cost" to be their "give me for free".

_____

_____

_____

_____

Any event that is free and open to the public is probably a good indication that you are invited. Sometimes you may not get a personal invite, but if you want to go, just show up. If you don't enjoy yourself, you didn't have to pay to attend, so you are free to leave at anytime.

_____
_____
_____
_____

Being BOLDER does not make you BETTER! Perhaps the BITTERNESS of others makes them think you are. But in some way you are because you don't carry around the weight of envy, jealously, strife, and bitterness. FREE YOURSELF!

_____
_____
_____
_____

Don't go anywhere or say anything without it being a part of your purpose. Time wasted is time desired when your time is up.

_____
_____
_____
_____

The Student Teacher Quotes

Pray for under shepherds because when they are wounded or killed, their sheep go astray and many end of being slaughtered.

_____
_____
_____
_____

You are not working for God. God already worked on behalf of you.

_____
_____
_____
_____

Before you fall, reach out and let Him catch you.

_____
_____
_____
_____

You are not as important to people as you think you are.
You are more important to God than you think or deserve.

Stop allowing people to accept and embrace your trash,
while they reject your treasure.

Fake-Christian is too nice of a word to describe an
unbeliever or pretender. You are Anti-Christ!

The Student Teacher Quotes

You never have to tell people what you are against, as long as you keep standing for what you believe.

_____
_____
_____
_____

As a believer, have you masked yourself as the laborer when you're really the harvest? Let someone minister to you so you too can be converted.

_____
_____
_____
_____

As a coach, have you masked yourself as the instructor when you're really the pupil? Let someone teach and coach you before you decide you want to be the instructor.

_____
_____
_____
_____

Don't grieve over a lie. Repent for the truth.

_____
_____
_____
_____

You are one testimony away from your breakthrough. You are one testimony away from your deliverance. You are one testimony away from your healing. You are one testimony away from overcoming. That one testimony is keeping you from freedom. FREE YOURSELF!

_____
_____
_____
_____

Dysfunctional relationships usually originate from dysfunctional families.

_____
_____
_____
_____

Some people will chase you until they catch you, to only throw you away once they got you.

___

Friends see, know, and address your mess. Friends walk with you through your mess. Friends address your mess so you don't stay in it. Friends pray for you to recover all once your mess is over. Friends are the ones who will cover your mess until you are strong enough to share the message and lesson learned from your mess. Friends don't run away from your mess. Friends celebrate with you when you come out of your mess. It is your messiness that can push friends away if you refuse to acknowledge or deal with your mess.

___

Don't give man too much credit.

If you follow people to find fault, there is fault in your finding and your following.

You should not want people to feel condemned. You should want them to feel convicted.

Stop focusing on the evil and share Jesus.

The Student Teacher Quotes

Any pastor that preaches and teaches the Word of God to make your soul come alive is worth the drive.

___

Stop crying over death and celebrate life.

___

What the enemy thought he would use to stain your name will be used as a badge of honor to showcase the power, faithfulness, and mercy of God.

At all cost, protect the anointing that cost you.

_____
_____
_____
_____

Faithfulness to God multiplies faithfulness to you.

_____
_____
_____
_____

There is a place of honor for our leaders, but after you have served your leaders, co-laborers, and church, go serve the sinner.

_____
_____
_____
_____

Be afraid of God's judgement, but never of His love.

_____
_____
_____
_____

When it is too hard to change, we just ask God to accept it. Instead of asking God to accept it, ask God to change you and accept the fact that the change God requires is you.

___

You do not need a title; you just need the power of The Holy Ghost.

___

Stop celebrating fornication by hosting, attending, and planning baby showers of unwed parents.

Do not be accountable to someone who is not accountable to someone else.

Your pure desires are dangerous to the enemy.

A professor, pastor, prophet, parent, or partner may miss it, but The Spirit of Truth never will.

Are you a fruit bearing friend, wolf in sheep's clothing friend, or a leaf bearing friend?

_____

_____

_____

_____

People can not tell you who to love; they can only tell you if it is right or wrong.

_____

_____

_____

_____

Any man who thinks a woman's sin is sexy needs deliverance. Ladies he is probably not the one you should marry. FREE YOURSELF!

_____

_____

_____

_____

Sin is sold at a cheap price. Salvation will cost you your life.

Things do not change when you speak your words; it changes when you speak God's words.

You are not rejected. You are redirected.

Don't be controlled by LUST.
(Locked Under Satanic Tyranny)

The Student Teacher Quotes

Whose identity have you hijacked? If it is not the Lord's, give it back.

_____

_____

_____

_____

Become a practitioner of prayer.

_____

_____

_____

_____

Find you a clean vessel who can cover you until you come out.

_____

_____

_____

_____

When our schools are governed by pride, it subtlety undermines the sovereignty of God.

God will keep you from being exposed until you can handle the cost of recovery.

I don't just want to shout. I want to be shaken, stirred, and shifted.

If you know God's precepts, you will hate every false way. On the contrary, if you do not know God's precepts, you will love every false way.

Leadership is hard. It just looks glamorous.

Deliverance is continual. Continue being daily delivered and set free.

The best revenge is to get in the Word of God.

Many may know you in the flesh, but they do not know you in the spirit.

Do not go to hell because of second hand hatred. Why hate someone based on the opinions and thoughts of others?

The Student Teacher Quotes

Be careful of those who befriend you and talk to you just so they can keep a track of what others are saying about them. They are eavesdroppers who are making sure they keep their name clean to you.

Some are young, fly, and saved, while others are young, fly, and sinners.

What used to stain your name will be what brings your name much gain. FREE YOURSELF!!

Comparison is a killer. It kills family relationships. It kills work relationships. It kills sibling relationships. It kills your self-esteem. Stop comparing. FREE YOURSELF!

People want your prayers but they don't want your Jesus.

Don't change because people do.

The Student Teacher Quotes

Your strengths sometimes exposes the weakness of others and they do not like it.

_____

_____

_____

_____

The world teaches you fourteen days can break a habit. In many cases, it has to take the finger of God to destroy the strongman in your life that seems to manifest shortly after your fourteen day surrender. It will take you a lifetime of changed behavior and new mindsets to be healed, delivered, set free, and forever changed.

_____

_____

_____

_____

When you're honest about it, God can fix it. When you keep it a secret, satan can use it against you.

_____

_____

_____

_____

People hang on to you when they think they will benefit from your success. People run away from your downfall when they think it will ruin their name.

___

Hidden Depression Shows!

___

You can never understand the depthless of who God is in your intellect. Remember your ways are not His and your thoughts aren't either.

The Student Teacher Quotes

Divine connections in your personal, business, and spiritual life will yield divine blessings. Reject and destroy that which wants you to connect and collaborate with the demonic.

Maturity teaches you that you don't change your mind about your commitment because other people don't fulfill theirs.

Live an open life. Open your life to God and his Word and watch Him live in you.

Simene' Walden

Sin literally can weigh you down.

When you leave, it makes room for someone or something else.

Some mothers rather make excuses for their sons instead of making them take responsibility for becoming a father.

The Student Teacher Quotes

If you mislead God's sheep, he will give them a new under-shepherd.

___

Don't take your anger and frustration out on the child of the adult that you are really angry with.

___

People will pay to promote their ignorance and sin.

Simene' Walden

Pray to God to keep your mouth shut and let Him speak for you.

There are seven things you can not buy: love, honor, respect, gratitude, appreciation, desire, and long- life.

If people talked about your sin in secret, they will whisper about your deliverance in public.

The Student Teacher Quotes

The work is in the world.

_____
_____
_____
_____

Have a lot to say when you know what to say.

_____
_____
_____
_____

Writers, sow your book into the lives of readers.

_____
_____
_____
_____

Don't give people advice you might get jealous of later.

_____
_____
_____
_____

There is no such thing as right retaliation. Retaliation is wrong. Sabotage is cruel and believers should not be partakers of either, especially with their friends.

___

You can't step into new territory with an old anointing.

___

You can never understand God fully with your intellect.

___

Retire your sin and do not go back to that job.

The Student Teacher Quotes

If you want a personal invite to a public event, you don't need to go.

_____

_____

_____

_____

Post with a purpose.

_____

_____

_____

_____

Don't get mad at the god you put before the one and only living God when they let you down.

_____

_____

_____

_____

There is never a good day to share bad news, but the Good News should always be shared on any given bad day.

Receive people the way God found them.

Don't give me the perception of a picture. Give me the reality of your life.

Do not let the fears of others be projected onto you.

Fear has a nasty odor that stays in the room. It has the power to cripple people for life.

Fear says, "I am ready to write but not ready to publish". There is a divine exchange that can be found when you allow the spirits of power, love, and a sound mind to take over.

Be mature enough to speak with salty lips.

Do not let your emotions fool you into making rash decisions.

___

Every strategy and tip that you see posted on social media is not for you to try.

___

Boldness has a sound and a melody. Is your sound off key? Does your sound need more practice? Does your sound need a new director? Or is your sound melodious to the Father?

___

The Student Teacher Quotes

Share contagious kindness.

_____
_____
_____
_____

Your words create your world. Speak life.

_____
_____
_____
_____

Attack the actions of people and not the person.

_____
_____
_____
_____

Be the answer to the problem and not the problem we are still seeking an answer to.

_____
_____
_____
_____

One's opinions and behaviors do not necessarily justify or make someone else's wrong.

Sometimes people don't have more to give you. Other times The Holy Spirit may speak to them and say that what they gave is all they need to give you.

Everything belongs to God; some people just happen to own and acquire more here.

The Student Teacher Quotes

Pity support is poor support. Do not support someone out of pity.

___

Poor correction equals poor leadership.

___

The church is a hospital for the sick. -Unknown

Some people need to be critique coaches. All they do is tell someone else how to live their lives. They should at least get paid for it.

___

Teachers your worth is not determined by the one observation and evaluation. FREE YOURSELF!

___

If you only talk to a friend when you need them, you are not their friend. You are a client and they need to start sending you an invoice.

The Student Teacher Quotes

Do not purchase from someone who can't produce the same results in their own lives.

_____
_____
_____
_____

Scream, shout, and declare, "I AM WALKING IN MY NOW. STAY TUNED TO MY NEXT"!

_____
_____
_____
_____

There are real people behind real titles. Get to know the person so you can stop making assumptions about their title.

_____
_____
_____
_____

Teacher talk is not teacher friendly because most of the time a teacher did not create it.

_____
_____
_____
_____

Your worst day is still someone else's best day. FREE YOURSELF!

_____
_____
_____
_____

If every believer that felt rejected, alone, isolated, or forsaken by family and friends would rally together, the body of Christ would be more unified and stronger than any organization created.

_____
_____
_____
_____

The Student Teacher Quotes

There is power in the prophetic and prayer.

Anyone you look up to should always be looking up to God.

Don't use your access but use the access.

Readers purchase more books from great writers.

Words of Gratitude

Thank you for your purchase and support. Please send your five- star review to thestudentteacher17@gmail.com. Any quote that you use on social media, please tag me in your post. God bless the works of your hands and may he establish, perfect, and complete the good work he has started in you.

Write down the names of ten people whom you can either gift this book to or who needs to read it.

1. _____
2. _____
3. _____
4. _____
5. _____
6. _____
7. _____
8. _____
9. _____
10. _____

www.ingramcontent.com/pod-product-compliance
Lightning Source LLC
Chambersburg PA
CBHW070630300426
44113CB00010B/1727